Encyclopedia Brown's Second Record Book Of Weird And Wonderful Facts

Encyclopedia Brown's Second Record Book Of Weird And Wonderful Facts

By Donald J. Sobol

Illustrated by
Bruce Degen

A YEARLING BOOK

Published by
Dell Publishing Co., Inc.
1 Dag Hammarskjold Plaza
New York, New York 10017

For information address Delacorte Press,
New York, New York.

Yearling ® TM 913705, Dell Publishing Co., Inc.

ISBN: 0-440-42421-6

Reprinted by arrangement with Delacorte Press

Printed in the United States of America

First Yearling printing—November 1982

CW

For Paul Feehan -

Acknowledgments

In preparing this book, I received help from many sources. I wish to express my gratitude to:

Larry Ayers of Healy, Kansas; Paul Babladelis of Cooks, Michigan; Albert Bourge of Bellevue, Washington; Tutt S. Bradford of Maryville, Tennessee; Larry Breer of Salina, Kansas; Lisa van Benthem of La Jolla, California; Margot M. J. van den Broek of The Hague, Netherlands; Woody Brown of Mountain View, California; Johnny Carter of Waco, Texas; John Crumpacker of San Francisco, California; J. Carrol Dadisman of Columbus, Georgia; Lin Dunn, Paul Feehan, and Richard and Cecy Rowen of Miami, Florida; James A. Foley of Hugo, Colorado; Joseph Gerencser of Milford, Indiana; Cleo Hill of Newark, New Jersey; George Hunter of Lantana, Florida; Claude Marsh of Saginaw, Michigan; A. R. Marschall of Washington, D.C.; Gary Ostrander of Seattle, Washington; Belinda

Rhoades Penny of Mayflower, Arkansas; Diane Perna of Rochester, New York; Linda S. Port of Syracuse, New York; David R. Smith of Burbank, California; Dorothy Mae Thomas of Fairbanks, Alaska; Warren F. Nardelle of New Orleans, Louisiana; Marion Tinsley of Tallahassee, Florida; Dennis Wepman of New York City; Richard Whitmer of Dorrance, Kansas; Morgan Wootten of Hyattsville, Maryland.

And my special thanks to Rose, my wife, who put up with a walking card file for four months.

—D.J.S.

Contents

Gym Dandies   1

One Lioners and Bushy Tales   42

Body English   65

Reading, Writing, and . . . Really?   83

Flabbergasting Facts   99

Aspirin Alley   118

Encyclopedia Brown's Second Record Book Of Weird And Wonderful Facts

Gym Dandies

Never once upon a mat. . . .

The country wasn't quite ready in 1979 for
Rhonda Bingham, 16, of Ballard, Washington.

A spunky 5-foot-2-inch, 115-pound blond sopho-

more, Rhonda was the only girl on a varsity wrestling team.

Competing for Bellevue High School, she went undefeated in all 3 of her matches. Her male opponents forfeited rather than wrestle her.

Oh, that sinking feeling. . . .

Daryl Moreau of New Orleans, Louisiana, a guard on the De La Salle High School basketball team, sank 126 consecutive free throws.

He began his record-busting streak on January 17, 1978, against Jesuit and ended it against the same team on January 9, 1979, when he missed on the last of 6 attempts.

"I was kind of surprised," said Daryl, 18, a 6-foot-1-inch, 171-pound senior. "It had been such a long time since I missed."

In 4 games in 1930, the Hugo (Colorado) High School football team scored 515 points while holding their opponents to 6.

The touchdown spree buried Burlington, 104–0; Flager, 106–0; Simla, 129–0; and Vona, 176–6.

High scorer for the year was halfback Ken Pearson

with 188 points. Against Vona he huffed and puffed for 72. Three other backs went well over 100 points, and a *guard* had 52.

Several days before the last game of the season, most of the 18 boys on the squad were weakened by an epidemic of dysentery. They were defeated by Canon City on Thanksgiving Day, 20–6, for the only loss in 11 games.

Ellen Minkow, a Syracuse University coed, was the first woman ever to enter an Intercollegiate Association of Amateur Athletes track meet. In the 1-mile walk at Princeton, New Jersey, in 1974, she showed her heels to 9 men, winning by 25 seconds in the time of 7:36.9.

I love you, waa, waa, waa. . . .
The Tulsa Roughnecks of the North American Soccer League grew tired of hearing criticism that they had failed to develop home-grown talent. They vowed to sign the first male born in Tulsa each year of the 1980s.

In January, 1980, the club signed its number 1 future player, Michael Ray Littlefield, age 3 days.

"A lot of Roughneck players haven't spoken English," a club official said, "and the kid doesn't either."

Soccer it to 'em, Michael!

Although it's not a contact sport, girls' gymnastics has an injury rate nearly as high as football's.

Playing for Kipps: After Aurora sank a lay-up to lead Kipp, 51–49, in a Kansas high school basketball game on January 28, 1964, the game was called with 15 seconds still left on the clock.

The score had been tied, 49–49, with less than

2 minutes remaining, when the last of junior guard Larry Breer's Kipp teammates fouled out. Since there were only 5 boys (and 12 girls) in the rural school, Breer, 16, had to battle the Aurora quintet alone.

In the next minute and 45 seconds, Breer, playing heroically, allowed but that one, go-ahead shot.

After Aurora scored, he was stranded at the baseline with no one to pass to. He planned to bounce the ball off an opposing player. But the Aurora team retreated to the far end of the court, and the game had to be halted.

The greatest margin by which a track-and-field record was ever broken was Michael Carter's 12-pound shot put of 81 feet 3½ inches in 1979. He beat the old national high school record by a phenomenal 12.5 percent.

Two weeks later Carter, 18, of Dallas, Texas, threw the 16-pound ball 67 feet 9 inches, another high school record.

Road games up in Alaska require more than your ordinary bus ride.

In order to play Bob Reeve High in girls' basketball in 1980, the Glennallen High team had to travel 1,490 miles.

A mare difference: A women's polo team was holding its own against a men's team at the West Hills Stables in Huntington, New York, in 1979, when one of the women's ponies scored a goal for the men. The gift gave the men a 3–2 win.

"It wasn't my pony," declared schoolgirl Jackie Chazey, 17, the team captain. "I was riding a mare. The pony that kicked the goal was a male."

WITH THE EYELASHES AND THE LIPSTICK THEY'LL NEVER KNOW IT'S YOU, JACK.

And now, not on tape, but live. . . .

Neither of the other 2 teams had entered the final event of the 1977 triangular women's track meet at Moorpark, California. But the Santa Barbara City College mile relay team still didn't win.

As Barbara Smith, the anchor runner, headed all

alone for the finish line, an excited teammate dashed onto the track and broke the tape. Santa Barbara was disqualified.

When Wilfredo Benitez defeated Antonio Cervantes in Puerto Rico on March 6, 1976, for the junior welterweight title, he became the youngest fighter ever to win a world boxing championship. He was 17.

Snatching defeat from victory. . . .

A 6-point win was turned into a 5-point loss in a high school basketball game in Los Angeles on December 4, 1979—after the game was over.

The "defeated" Daniel Murphy players had left the court when Glenn Marx, coach of the "victorious" Notre Dame team, had words with the 2 officials. They called a series of technical fouls on him.

Under high school rules, a coach must leave the court after receiving 3 technical fouls. If he refuses to leave, he may incur any number of fouls.

Marx had 12 fouls laid on him.

Herb Simon, 16, did the shooting for Daniel Murphy. He made 8 straight, missed 1, hit 3 more. The 11-point play swung a 61–67 defeat into a 72–67 win.

Lights, camera, action: Linda Williams, a right fielder for Wheatley High School, became the first girl to play on a boys' varsity baseball team in Texas.

On hand to watch her every move were 4 TV camera crews, 15 newspaper reporters, and 300 fans.

Under such pressure, Linda struck out, grounded out, and walked in 3 trips to the plate against Sterling High. She committed a first-inning error that allowed 4 runs to score.

Footnote to history: The game was played March 29, 1978, and Sterling, the unhistoric team, won, 7–0.

NO MORE INTERVIEWS DURING THE GAME, PLEASE!

'Tis better to have played and tossed. . . .

Although his Maggie Walker High basketball team was assured of victory over George Wythe High in a game in Richmond, Virginia, on February 4, 1978, Michael Gibson couldn't resist a last slam dunk.

The score was 66–65 with 4 seconds left when Michael soared and slammed—into the wrong basket.

He *missed*.

Lucky? Yes . . . no . . . *groan*. Wythe's Paul Pressey snatched the rebound and scored at the buzzer for a 67–66 win.

The Howard sisters of San Bernardino, California, like to run.

Arta, 17; Sherri, 16; Tina, 15; and Denean, 14,

made up the San Gorgonio High School's mile relay team in 1979. They smashed the national girls' high school record by 3.5 seconds with a clocking of 3:44.1. At the same meet, Sherri established the national girls' 440-yard record with a time of 53.65.

The van Benthem triplets of La Jolla, California, like to throw.

In 1974, at the age of 14, Lisa, Lorelei, and Lynne were ranked 1, 2, and 3 respectively in the javelin throw for girls 14 and 15 years old. All 3 won scholarships to the University of Southern California.

The first winner of an Olympic gold medal in women's springboard diving was tiny (65 pounds) Aileen Riggen, 14, of the United States, in 1920.

Four years later she became the first competitor in the history of the Olympics to win medals in both diving and swimming—a silver in springboard and a bronze in the 100-meter backstroke.

Fastest shooter in the West. . . .

Danny Heater scored 135 points to lead Burnsville to a 173–43 victory over Widen in a high school basketball game on January 26, 1960, in West Virginia.

Heater hit on 53 of 70 field goal attempts and 29 of 41 free throws. His 82 points in the second half included 55 in the final 10 minutes. He took time off to grab 32 rebounds.

Block Buster: When Traverse City frosted Saginaw by 48–0 in the opening round of the 1979 Michigan High School ice hockey tournament, the star of the game was Tom Szcyzypka, 17.

If you guessed Tom was high scorer for Traverse City, you're wrong. Tom was the loser's goalie.

Altogether, he survived the bombardment of 129 shots. And if he let in 48, no one at the game will forget the number he blocked—81.

On September 7, 1977, Cindy Nicholas, 20, of Scarborough, Canada, became the first woman swimmer to accomplish a round-trip, nonstop crossing of

the English Channel. Her time of 19 hours and 55 minutes slashed an astounding 10 hours and 5 minutes off the old record, set by a man, Jon Erikson, of Chicago, in 1975.

A woman's home is not her castle. . . .
Chess watchers maintain that women mature more quickly in the game, but their ability declines sooner.

When the University of Miami football team lost to Florida State, 40–23, on October 22, 1979, wide receiver Larry Brodsky twice had to tackle a defender who had intercepted a pass.
He thus tied for the lead for the most unassisted tackles by a Miami player—2.

Mayday! Mayday!

By the 12-mile mark in the Midnight Sun Marathon in Fairbanks, Alaska, on June 14, 1975, Paul D. Vanture had forged comfortably into the lead. He seemed assured of winning for the second straight year.

But at the 20-mile turnaround, Marian May, one of the few women in the field of 53 runners, had closed to within 50 yards. In the next mile, May, 21, caught and passed him.

Vanture responded by running the race of his life,

and in fact broke his own record, set the year before.

Yet not for him were the victory cheers.

May had crossed the finish line nearly 2 minutes earlier.

It was the first time a woman had outrun all the men in a major marathon. What's more, her clocking, 3:02:41, gave her the Midnight Sun record.

IT SAVES A LOT OF ROCKET FUEL THIS WAY.

Someone finally figured it out: Americans jog about 17 billion miles a year—enough for 90 round trips to the sun.

What has no brakes, can go 50 miles an hour downhill, and in 1978 was ridden by 140,000 people straight to hospital emergency rooms? Answer: a skateboard.

English golfers of the 18th century were an aristocratic lot. They customarily started each hole with a cup of tea. Thus the expression, "tea off."

When the lords realized that so much fluid was water-logging their swing, they abandoned the tradition, and "tea" became "tee."

Check this out: In 1952 Marion Tinsley, 15, of Columbus, Ohio, entered Ohio State University and put himself through college by staging exhibitions at checkers. He would play 20 opponents at once and beat them all—blindfolded.

When he was world checkers champ, a 1978 match against a computer at Duke University fell through. It was discovered the machine could plan only 8 or 9 moves ahead.

Tinsley could think 30 to 40 moves ahead.

HOW ABOUT YOU WEAR A BLINDFOLD NEXT GAME?

Coach Larry Ayers ordered a third down punt "just to see if we could get away with one." It worked, the only punt of 7 that his Healy (Kansas) High School 8-man football team didn't have blocked in a game on October 5, 1979, against Dorrance.

Dorrance, which won 107–0, didn't have to punt.

There are an estimated 141,000 tennis courts in the United States.

True grit: Dennis Rainear, 26, of Midland, Michigan, ran the final 16 miles of the 1978 Grand Valley Marathon in Allendale, Michigan, after being struck in the head by a .22 caliber bullet.

Rainear thought he had been hit with a rock. Looking around, he saw no one suspicious.

He kept going. Undaunted by a lump on the top of his skull the size of a goose egg, by blurred vision and ringing in his ears, he finished the race in 3 hours and 9 minutes.

After the bullet was removed, he could only guess that he was the victim of a hunter who "shot at a squirrel or something and missed."

Warming up in sunny California. . . .

The 3 high schools that have sent the most baseball players to the majors are all from the Golden State: Oakland Technical with 18, Long Beach Poly with 17, and Los Angeles Fremont with 15.

For 2 seasons the football team of Big Bay de Noc High School in Michigan achieved fame because of its eggshell offense. The team failed to score in 15 straight games, a national high school record.

Then in the very last quarter of the 1979 season, Big Bay finally tallied on a 1-yard plunge by Ron Collins. He looked around for a penalty flag. There was none.

The other members of the team and their 250 die-

hard fans stared wide-eyed at the scoreboard. "So that's what a six looks like," muttered one father.

Joy piled upon joy when quarterback Mike Popour passed to Collins for a 2-point conversion. Big Bay lost the game, played on October 20 against North Dickinson, and so extended its losing streak to 25. But that was of small moment.

The 8 points meant Big Bay had been outscored by only 864 to 8 in its last 16 games.

But you can't lose 'em all. In the 1980 season opener Big Bay defeated Brimley, 14–0.

But no football team in high school history ever rivaled the single season performance of the stingless Bees of Bethel High of Brandt, Ohio.

On the way to becoming a legend, Bethel lost all of its 10 games in 1974 by the nail-biting scores of 40–0, 53–0, 92–0, 89–0, 50–0, 56–0, 36–0, 33–0, 46–0, and 49–0.

The 89–0 game was mercifully called after 3 minutes of the third quarter. In the 56–0 cliff-hanger, Bethel's opponent started attempting field goals on first down.

Despite being outclassed, not a player quit the team after the opening game. The one-sided contests were tougher on the fans.

"Games Will Be Played, Unhappy Bee Fans

Told," announced one newspaper after the first 5 shellackings.

Admitted a cheerleader, "Toward the end of the year only the cheerleaders and the band were cheering. And some of the band quit, too."

William "Blinky" Rodriguez and his wife, Lili, like to slug it out, but not with each other.

On November 16, 1979, they fought in Los Angeles, the first time as far as anyone knows that a husband and wife boxed on the same card. Both won.

For Blinky, a middleweight, it was his first professional fight. He was paid $400.

Lili, a veteran of 11 professional fights and the California women's flyweight champion, did better. She took home $1,000.

"When you have a title, you can ask for more money," she observed.

Jay Helgerson, 24, of Foster City, California, became the first person to complete a marathon a week for 52 weeks.

His fastest time was 2:46:0, and he ran the last 45 races in under 3 hours each. The 5-foot-6, 130 pounder ended his super-footed feat by sprinting across the finish line (wearing number 52) at the Houston Marathon on January 19, 1980.

As a teen-ager, Benjamin Franklin toyed with the idea of becoming a swimming instructor. In one of his earliest experiments, he sailed a kite while in the water and let himself be pulled along by the wind.

Mandy Joslin of Seattle, Washington, calculated that each knee had to flex 4,250,000 times in her bicycle ride across Canada from Vancouver to Newfoundland.

With 4 minutes left in the basketball game, Geannine Griffith, 14, stepped to the foul line. She had 2 free throws. She made the first but missed the second.

"If I'd missed them both, I'd just have died," she said.

The point kept her Harvard–St. George High School team from being skunked by Chicago Latin on February 14, 1978. The final score was 117–1.

Geannine's coach, Lynn Hudson, didn't see the 1-pointer. "To tell the truth," she said, "things were so bad I had my eyes closed most of the game."

Harvard–St. George had only 10 girls in school, and 6 were on the team. Only one could dribble.

The single point kept Chicago Latin from racking up a national girls' high school record. The biggest shutout is believed to be 106–0 in a 1931 game in Oklahoma.

New Amateur Athletic Union records were set in all 14 events in the 1964 AAU indoor swimming championships in New Haven, Connecticut.

Defense . . . *Deeefense*!

McLennan Community College and Kilgore Junior College totaled 334 points in a single basketball game, the most points ever scored—high school, college, or professional. The game was played in Kilgore, Texas, on November 13, 1979, and lasted 3 hours and 15 minutes.

After trailing 59–54 at the half, McLennan tied

the game at 117–117, sending it into 4 overtimes. The teams deadlocked at 139–139 after the first overtime, at 151–151 after the second, and at 157–157 after the third. McLennan finally won, 169–165.

For batter or worse: A women's slow-pitch softball game in the Lansing, Michigan, Class C City League in 1978 was prudently called after 2 innings with the score 53–0.

The losers, whose 16 errors didn't help, apparently never expected to earn fame on the diamond. Their name: The Unknowns.

No-need-to-leave-the-kitchen department. According-ing to golf writer Peter Dobereiner, you can shut your eyes and tell if it's a woman hitting a drive.

"When a woman hits the ball off a tee, the sound is 'woosh, plop.' When a man hits one, the sound is 'whizz, tok.' You can duplicate the sound of a woman's shot by taking a hard-boiled egg, removing the shell, and hurling it against a wall."

Dodgers hurler Sandy Koufax had one of the few perfect seasons in the major leagues. As a 19-year-old rookie in 1955, he came to bat 12 times and fanned 12 times.

A time to try her soles. . . .

In what is generally regarded as the best-ever track performance by a girl her age, Elizabeth Onyambu, 12, of Nyana Province, Kenya, running barefoot, won the women's 1,500 meters in 4:23.18 at the 1979 Jomo Kenyatta Invitational at Nairobi.

Point spread: Some basketball teams have scored more points. Others have scored fewer. But none approach the high-low wins of the quintet from Essex County College of Newark, New Jersey.

On January 19, 1974, Essex romped over Englewood Cliffs, 210–67. Four years later, on February 18, 1978, Essex inched past Ocean County College, 8–4.

Shy, auburn-haired Diane Perna, 9, of Rochester, New York, scored 48 goals and had 14 assists in leading her Parkland girls' soccer team to a 9–1 record in 1979.

Diane, a right wing with a mean hook kick and the ability to read defenses, scored 8 goals in one game and 7 in another.

Yo hum: The yo-yo comes from a deadly weapon used in the Philippines for hundreds of years. It was introduced into the United States as a toy in 1929.

James R. Richard of Ruston, Louisiana, hit 4 consecutive home runs and drove in 10 runs in a high school baseball game as Lincoln walloped Jonesboro Jackson, 48–0, in 1969. That same year Richard, a pitcher, had a 0.00 earned run average.

A decade later, in 1978, the 6-foot-8-inch fireballer became the first National League right-hander to strike out more than 300 batters in a single season.

Super hooper: Sylvia Wilson, 18, of Haines City, Florida, broke 11 school records and tied another as she led the University of Miami women's basketball team in both scoring and rebounding in the 1979–1980 season.

The 6-foot, 175-pound freshman could palm a basketball in each hand simultaneously. In strength tests, she did better than all the school's male golfers, tennis players, and soccer players and most of the swimmers and baseball players.

OH YEAH? HOW ABOUT A PIE-BAKING CONTEST!

Yale University became the first college football team to win 700 games when it defeated Cornell, 23–20, in the final minutes on November 3, 1979.

Three points was also the margin of its very first victory—a 3–0 squeaker against Columbia on November 16, 1872.

Steve Mordecai of Gardendale, Alabama, compiled the best record of any United States high school wrestler. He finished his scholastic career in 1978 undefeated in 141 matches. He had won state championships in 4 weight classes: 95, 105, 119, and 132 pounds.

"Some guys are funny. They actually back off," said Patti Tuckfield, 17, the lone girl on the Coral Park (Florida) High School water polo team in 1978. "If they accidentally touch me, they say, 'I'm sorry.' "

Rob Aliuni, 16, who played alongside Patti in the Ram defense; remarked enviously, "She can get away with murder, and in some games she has."

Wilt Chamberlain set a National Basketball Association record that took the combined efforts of all the other players 3 decades to break.

When Freeman Williams of the San Diego Clippers scored 51 points against Phoenix on January 19, 1980, it was only the 123rd time in the 31-year history of the NBA that a player other than Chamberlain had scored 50 points in a game.

In his 14-year career, Chamberlain had scored 50 points 122 times.

Officials' laps(e): Norway's Greta Waitz ran 3,000 meters in 8:51 in San Francisco on January 5, 1980, well under the women's indoor record of 8:57.6.

But hold the record book! The judges had flubbed the lap count. Waitz and the rest of the field had covered 3,000 meters plus 1 lap—an extra 160 yards.

The judges decided to call the race 3,000 meters anyway and recorded everyone's final time—giving Waitz a sluggish 9:15.1.

The standard golf ball has 336 dimples.

In 1966 the Chargers of the Sunnyvale (California) Little League wound up in the cellar. Where else to hide from the other teams in the league—the Lions, the Cobras, the Wildcats, the Panthers, and the Dragons?
Watta zoo!

An 8-man shell can be rowed only about 25 percent faster than a single scull.

Get up and bar the door. . . .
In a high school football game in Miami, Florida, on November 9, 1979, Southwest took a 6–0 lead against Coral Gables and lost, 56–6.

Friends to everyone: On February 15, 1973, the basketball team of Friendsville (Tennessee) Academy ended 6 winless seasons by beating St. Camillus Academy of Corbin, Kentucky, 64–43.

The Friendsville streak, begun February 7, 1967, had reached 138 defeats in a row, a record that may never be seriously threatened.

St. Camillus had brought its own modest losing string of 48 into the game. The following year it gave up basketball for soccer.

Gary Gerencser, 13, of Milford, Indiana, may never win the National Open, but you can mount an argument that he was the best golfer off the tee in 1978. He made holes-in-one on 3 consecutive rounds.

On Saturday, June 3, at the Parmore Golf Course in New Paris, he aced the 188-yard ninth hole with a 4-wood. On Sunday he aced the 115-yard seventh hole with a 9-iron. On Monday he moved to nearby South Shore Golf Course in Syracuse and aced the 140-yard fifth hole with a 4-iron.

Gary cooled off for 6 days. Then, on June 11, he returned to Parmore and aced the seventh hole again.

Root beer for the house.

That's my Les, the big shot. . . .

A miracle shot by Les Henson enabled Virginia

Tech to nip Florida State 79–77 in a basketball game on January 21, 1980.

Henson grabbed a rebound near the baseline, spun, took a step, and heaved the ball down court as the buzzer sounded. It swished through the net—89 feet 3 inches away—without touching the rim or the backboard, making it the longest 2-pointer ever.

Putting the club before the course: Two psychologists have been successful in teaching golf to beginners by going from short to long.

Students start with the putter and work up, club by club, to the driver.

In a district elimination football game between Palmetto and South Miami High Schools in Miami,

Florida, on November 20, 1978, the 4 officials lost sight not only of the ball, but of a touchdown.

A whistle blew the play dead after running back Allen Lawrence of Palmetto was thrown for a small loss. Lawrence didn't have the ball.

Quarterback Ritchie Bennett, after faking the handoff, had, unnoticed, spun over from the 1-yard line with what should have been the go-ahead touchdown.

South Miami scored later and won, 7–0.

The closest ski race was the 15 kilometers (9.4 miles) in the 1980 Olympics at Lake Placid, New York, on February 17. Thomas Wassberg of Sweden won in 41:57.63—1/100 of a second faster than Juha Mieto of Finland.

The closest boys' high school basketball game was played between Boone Trail and Angier on February 29, 1964, in Mamers, North Carolina. Boone Trail won, 56–54, in a record 13 overtimes.

The closest girls' high school basketball game was played between Melvin and Sibley on February 21, 1979, in Sheldon, Iowa. At the end of regulation play, the score was tied, 0–0.

Melvin won, 4–2, on a 6-foot jump shot by Deb Mouw with a minute left in the fourth overtime.

The closest sled race was the 1978 Iditarod Trail Sled Dog Race over more than 1,000 miles of rugged Alaskan countryside from Anchorage to Nome.

Dick Mackey's lead dog reached the finish line on March 19 in 14 days, 18 hours, 52 minutes, and 24 seconds—a second ahead of Rick Swenson's.

First glass, all the way: To fire up his football players before sending them out to meet unbeaten St. Helena on October 5, 1979, Coach Emelio Tesei of Live Oak (Louisiana) High School played a tape of a General George S. Patton speech.

Stirred to a fever pitch by those fighting words, 3 players charged through a glass door and suffered cuts.

Live Oak then lost, 36–14.

Between December of 1961 and December of 1976, DeMatha Catholic High School in Hyattsville, Maryland, won 124 straight home basketball games.

L'Chayim: Nick Akers, a distance runner, changed his name in March, 1980, to Nick Vladivar after the Vladivar Vodka Company, which helped sponsor his Cayman Islands Olympic team.

The most unusual high school triple threat was 5-foot-5, 125-pound Belinda Rhoades of Mayflower, Arkansas.

As a junior in 1976, Belinda, 16, was a cheerleader at Mayflower High. The next year she was crowned homecoming queen and lettered as end for the boys' football team.

She was thrown only one pass during the season.

It fell incomplete, but the opposition was penalized 15 yards for holding her.

Stand clear, the Israelis have discovered skiing. . . .

They attack the steep, dangerous slopes of Mount Hermon with typical Israeli fearlessness—usually unslowed by skiing lessons.

The rat-tat-tat of Syrian machine-gun practice less than a mile away bothers the daredevils not one christie. Neither do the rocks and barbed wire lying half-buried in the snow. Nonskiers add a challenge by cluttering the runs on homemade sleds, plastic sheets, boards, and toilet seats.

Bad visibility, icy conditions, cuts, bruises, and broken bones cannot stem the enthusiasm or the mayhem. One morning a ski-lift operator warned a group that the runs were especially dangerous.

Replied a skier: "What do you care? At the end of the day, just collect the bodies."

Sprinter Evelyn Ashford turned the 50-meter dash at the 1980 Examiner Games in San Francisco into a trio of happenings.

She: 1) finished dead last; 2) bettered her own women's American indoor record of 6.26 by 2/100 of a second; 3) had the record disallowed because she ran against a field of 7 men.

The expression "to win hands down" comes from horse racing. The jockey relaxes his grip on the reins and drops his hands when victory is certain.

One up on Robin Hood: Tommy Thompson of Bloomfield, Iowa, accomplished archery's first triple.

Shooting a group of 10 arrows, he put his first arrow into the bull's-eye, his second into the first, and his fourth into the second.

Thompson, the defending Professional Archers Association indoor champion, used a recurve bow with no release aids. He made his 3-stacker from 60 feet at the PAA tournament at Norfolk, Nebraska, on November 10, 1979.

Net worth: The popularity of tennis peaked in the United States in 1976, when sales of racquets set a record of $184 million. Enthusiasm declined when it was discovered that more than expensive equipment kept the ball in play.

Billy Duggleby of the Phils was the only man to hit a grand slam home run in his first time at the plate in the majors. The unique sock occurred in the second inning of a game against the New York Giants on April 21, 1898.

The 1974 Athlete of the Year award at Seattle University in Washington was given to the entire women's track team, which didn't win a meet.

The team consisted of a single athlete, Liane Swegle, 21, a nursing student. During the season she took 6 firsts and a second and had a 2:07.4 time in her specialty, the 880-yard run.

In 1900 rowing was added to the Olympics. That year, there were 1,505 athletes registered for the Paris games—plus a mystery boy whose name and exact age will never be known.

During the coxswain-with-pairs heats, Herman Brockmann was coxswain for the Amsterdam-based Dutch crew. His body weight, however, seemed a heavy bar to victory in the finals. In the emergency, a small French boy, between 7 and 10 years old, was drafted in his place.

The boy calmly shouted the Dutch crew to a split-second victory over the French, 7:34.2 to 7:34.4. He thus became the youngest Olympic winner ever.

But after the race he disappeared into the crowd, and no one knows to this day if he ever received his gold medal.

One Lioners
and Bushy Tales

Rodney Fluery of Mountain, California, bit a rattle-snake to death in 1971 after the snake had bitten him and his dog.

Pigeons, which have keen eyesight and a long attention span, are being trained for sea rescues.

Strapped to the underside of a helicopter, the pigeons peck at a switch connected to a light in the cockpit when they spot yellow, orange, or red—the colors of life rafts, life vests, and flares.

The lion is the only big cat that chooses to live with his family.

Young giraffes can grow as much as half an inch per hour.

He knows the answer today but the quiz is tomorrow.

Chimpanzees learn faster than orangutans and gorillas, but they are apt to forget sooner.

Timberrrr! In 1975 alone, bugs destroyed enough board feet of forest timber to construct more than 900,000 homes.

Pound for pound, a man can outpull a horse.

Some accident of selective breeding is blamed for the fact that most ranch-raised minks are deaf.

Male tarantulas are smaller but faster than females, and they need their speed. After mating, a female will eat the male for lunch.

Drink to me only with thine. . . .

Some fruits ferment on the vine or in an animal's stomach. The result is tipsy wildlife.

—In Florida robins that gobble pyracantha berries bang into other robins or into telephone poles. Overripe nectar causes bees to bumble about with the staggers.

—Elephants in South Africa get looped and engaged in drunken charges after munching the fruit of the marula tree. In Sweden birds flop around on the shoulders of roads after downing fermented rowanberries.

—Hunters and collectors on the island of Mauritius in the Indian Ocean avoid wobbly pink pigeons. The plant that makes them giddy reacts to water in the bird's system and forms a poison—cyanide.

No natural fiber is stronger than spider silk, which, size for size, is stronger than steel and comes in at least 7 varieties.

Current efforts to preserve rare animals may not be sufficient, and so 2 Russian biologists have proposed a gene bank.

Cell samples from endangered species would be deep-frozen so that creatures could be reconstructed later if they became extinct.

Make mine an ice-gene coon.

Seagulls are the most widely distributed birds in the world because they can live on land or sea and drink either fresh- or saltwater.

Cotton tale: Rabbits can produce from 8 to 14 babies every 71 days.

One of the most spectacular newcomers to the animal world is the ape Shawn-Shawn, who was born in 1975.

Her parents are a male gibbon and a female siamang. They are farther apart genetically than great apes and human beings.

The amazing birth occurred in 1975 at Atlanta's Grant Park Zoo, where the gibbon and siamang shared the same cage.

Called "siabon," the hybrid Shawn-Shawn resembles a siamang in face and body. She does not, however, have the throat sac characteristic of a siamang, and perhaps that is the reason she was rejected by her mother after 3 months.

Good ol' boa: In a battle between a rattlesnake and a boa constrictor, pick the boa. The antitoxins in its system make it immune to the rattler's poison.

This is no yoke: Mother turkeys stand up while laying, and if the eggs survive the average 10-inch fall, Papa sometimes tries to break them.

Few Chinese keep pets, which may explain why Chinese kids on a class trip to the zoo stare at a cat or pigeon. Otherwise, Chinese zoos are much like American zoos.

The most deadly creature in nature's domain is not the lion or the shark, but the common Old World rat.

It carries diseases that have killed more humans than all the wars of mankind.

It spreads trichinosis, tularemia, and rabies. Its fleas still carry the bubonic plague; its lice, typhus.

And it contributes to food shortages throughout the world by destroying billions of dollars worth of crops.

Why, the dirty rat . . . !

An oyster can alternate its sex several times a season.

A 10-year study in California found that only 1 in 13 dogs stays with its original owner unless the owner is a breeder or the person who brought it into the world.

My heart belongs to Daddy. . . .
Alsopdale Sunbeam II, a Holstein bull renowned in international stud circles for having sired 200,000 offspring, died in London, England, in 1979 at age 14.

In 1979 scientists at the University of Lund in Sweden discovered that earthworms feel pain.

A Yale University professor, Dr. William Bennett, has calculated that a trillion monkeys, each hitting 10 keys on a typewriter per second, would need a trillion times longer than the universe is old to reproduce Shakespeare's famous line "To be, or not to be: that is the question."
And how long for the answer?

Wasps and hornets are extremely nearsighted. So if you keep fairly still and ignore them, they will usually go away.

I'll fly night roach, thank you. . . .

A pet shop in Station Road, Beeston, England, sells giant cockroaches—the 3-inch African variety —as pets.

"Apart from hissing a bit when they are angry, you couldn't wish for nicer pets," says the shop owner. "We stroke them when they crawl over us, but my wife doesn't like them in her hair. My son and I don't mind."

In New Zealand the law requires a dog owner to take his pet for a walk at least once every 24 hours.

In 90 percent of all bird species, males and females have but one mate. Among the species of mammals, only 3 percent take a single mate.

During a debate in 1979 over whether to retain the bluefish as the New Jersey state fish, Senator David Friedland pointed out that the bluefish was not native-born and was cannibalistic.

The fish chosen, he said, ought to be able to survive in the state's polluted waters. Further, it should have the decency to remain in the state if it is elected.

"The only proper fish for New Jersey is the gefilte fish," said Friedland. "It meets all the tests I have laid down. Once it arrives, it stays. It's inert. It just lays there sopping up sauce."

Despite such logic, the bluefish was retained as the state fish by a vote of 36 to 1.

You can be a star, baby. . . .
Chimpanzees like television, especially action and western shows.

A hole to hiss in: When disturbed, the hissing cockroach earns its name by forcing air through the breathing holes in the side of its body.

In racing, a filly is not called a mare until she is 5 years old.

The first Seeing Eye dog in the United States was named Kiss.

This'll gill you: The *Anabas scandens*, or "Indian fish," can store water in its gills. Thus, it can leave bodies of water that are drying up and move across land to deeper ones.

A male penguin may court a female by offering her small pebbles. If the gifts are accepted, he knows he has won her favor.

Chips, a combination of husky, German shepherd, and collie, was the only animal to win a Purple Heart and a Silver Star in World War II.

Trained as a sentry dog and assigned to the Third Infantry Division, Chips served in the North African, Mediterranean, and European Theaters of Operations.

While in Sicily he broke away from his handler

and attacked an enemy pillbox: He seized 1 soldier and forced the 4-man crew to surrender. He was also credited with alerting his unit on several occasions to enemy soldiers, causing their capture.

His medals were later taken away owing to a public outcry against awarding such high honors to a dog.

Anyone can play. . . .
When a gorilla beats its chest, it is showing curiosity and not a readiness to attack. In the young, chest-thumping is an invitation to play.

The kind of flea that is fond of human beings can long-jump 13 inches. Taking off, its rate of acceleration is 30 times the g force that a human can survive without losing consciousness.

The giraffe is the only animal that can fall 18 feet without having to climb something first.

Talk about hangups: Bats hang upside down because it hurts them to stand upright. Their thighs are undersized.

My son the platypus: When the Brookfield Zoo near Chicago needed to raise money, it launched a scheme whereby anyone could "adopt" an animal by donating money, though the animal stayed in the zoo.

Biggest fund-raiser, to everyone's surprise, was Olga, 19, a 1-ton Atlantic walrus that delighted in squirting water at onlookers.

A pig has 44 teeth. So don't squeal on him.

In 1765 John Ellis discovered that sponges were animals.

Humans and pigs are the only mammals that get sunburned.

WE RECOMMEND THE HOUSE EUCALYPTUS —
A LIGHT BOUQUET AND A FRUITY FLAVOR.

The koala bear isn't interested in drinking. It gets all the water it needs from eating the leaves of the eucalyptus tree.

In the United States more than twice as many persons are killed by the sting of bees, hornets, fire ants, and wasps as are killed by snakebites.

By using all its 5,000 nostrils, a bee can smell an apple tree 2 miles away.
Beelieve it or not.

The creature with the largest eyes is the giant squid. Each eye is as big as a basketball.

Monkeys are found in every tropical country except Australia.

Most birds avoid darkness. But more than half the world's mammals are active by night rather than by day.

In 1979 the brontosaurus's head rolled. Scientists decided that the snub-nosed skulls atop the skeletons in museums were pure wrongheadedness and replaced them with a more slender, longer model.

KIND OF A PREHISTORIC FACELIFT!

The British are among the most devoted pet owners. The 46 million of them share their small island with 4 million dogs, 6 million cats, 8 million caged birds, and an untold number of aquarium fish.

Bear this in mind: It's against the law to wrestle a bear in Missouri because the bear "might suffer torn tendons or broken cartilage."

A really gabby rooster can crow 85 times in half an hour.

It looked like the end for "Dr. Spock."

On February 23, 1978, the 12-year-old, 300-pound bottle-nosed dolphin swallowed a 3-inch pointed bolt left by a diver in the dolphin tank at Marine World USA outside San Francisco.

The next day veterinarian technician Ron Swallow tried reaching down and pulling the bolt from the first of Dr. Spock's 3 stomachs. He came up 9 inches short.

"What we need is a tall basketball player," someone suggested.

Clifford Ray, the Warrior's center, was in town recovering from a leg injury. He agreed to donate his 3-foot-9-inch arm reach to the cause.

His fingernails were trimmed. His right arm was

scrubbed and then greased so that his 16-inch biceps would slip down Dr. Spock's throat.

The operation had to be done quickly. After 3 minutes, Dr. Spock's breathing would be impaired.

As Ray started his shooting arm downward, onlookers kidded him about the demand for one-armed players in the NBA.

The clock ticked . . . 1 minute . . . 2 minutes. Ray kept running into folds of the stomach. But neither he nor the dolphin choked.

After 2½ minutes Ray's face lighted up. "I've got it!" he shouted.

With 5 seconds to spare, he withdrew the bolt.

For centuries the Malaysians have employed the world's cheapest labor to harvest coconuts—trained monkeys.

On a cold day a chickadee eats its own weight in food to keep warm.

Down to earth: The mole can tunnel through nearly 300 feet of earth every day.

Show me the way to go home—again. . . .
Twenty thousand homing pigeons started in the 1972 North Road Federation of Pigeon Fanciers' annual race. Five hundred finished. The rest of the 19,500 vanished along the 150-mile course in Yorkshire, England.

Fill 'er up: An elephant must drink 50 gallons of water a day just to stay alive.

Machine age: In the 19th century a Scotsman named David Hutton invented a tiny mill, powered by a mouse, for twisting twine. His plan to expand the model into a full-scale product using 10,000 mice was cut short by his death.

Now, see here. . . .
Contact lenses are bringing peace to the chicken coop.
"Wearing lenses helps prevent the chicken fights

and death that happen so often on chicken farms," says Dr. Darral Clarke, a professor at Brigham Young University.

The lenses actually make the chickens' eyesight worse by reducing their depth of focus to about 6 inches. With vision blurred, they can't tell the barnyard big shots from the underdogs, and so have difficulty in establishing a pecking order.

"Moreover," says Dr. Clarke, "the chickens have to walk around with bent heads, a sign of submissiveness, in order to find food."

Fido, a name often given to dogs, means "faithful" in Latin.

It's against the law to hunt camels in Arizona.

You may yet see a mammoth lumbering about a zoo.

Russian scientists are currently examining Dima, a frozen baby mammoth discovered in an icy Siberian riverbed in June, 1977.

If they find living cells or cells that were not damaged when Dima froze 40,000 years ago, the scientists will try to clone a cell and join it to a sex cell (probably an egg) from an elephant.

This would then be implanted in the elephant. Eighteen or 20 months afterward, it is hoped, the world would behold the first mammoth to walk the earth in 10,000 years.

Thanks to backyard feeders, birds are going to seed and not south for the winter. As a result, some species are becoming extinct.

During the summer birds grow used to freeloading. Thinking they have found a steady source of food, they forsake the age-old flight south.

Then homeowners grow bored with the daily job of refilling the feeders. The birds are left to starve in the cold.

In Illinois the state's Carolina wrens and mockingbirds are already close to extinction. The danger to other birds throughout the north is increasing.

Farkle, a cat who lives in Annapolis, Maryland, got a credit card in his own name in 1979.

"With the rough company he keeps, Farkle shouldn't have to rely on cash," said his owner, who guaranteed the account.

Prompt payment of his first charge, a vet's bill, raised Farkle's credit limit. It also snowed him with solicitations, including one from a yacht broker.

Bigfoot, a creature that hasn't been proved to exist, has been put on the protected list by the state of California.

The camel is the only plant-eating animal with a meat-eater's teeth.

Cats and gorillas need 14 hours of sleep out of every 24. Short-tailed shrews and elephants get by on 2.

A customs service dog can sniff 1,000 pieces of mail an hour and alert its handler to the presence of unlawful drugs. The same dog can sniff through a car in 4 to 6 minutes.

A man would need half an hour to search a car by hand and a week to go through 1,000 pieces of mail.

Where have all the goldfish gone?

Four Florida pet shops mistakenly sold 23 savage piranhas in 1976 to Tampa fish fanciers.

For 550 bees to produce just 1 pound of honey, they would have to suck the nectar from 2.5 million flowers.

The king cobra is the only animal in the world besides man capable of killing an elephant.

Body English

Electrical waves given off by the brain have been hooked up to run a toy train.

The importance of the thumb to humans is shown by the fact that the area of the brain controlling it is almost as large as the area controlling the hip and leg.

Your body burns calories just warming the cold air that you inhale.

So if you're looking for a way to lose weight without exercising or sweating, spend time in temperatures of 40 degrees below zero. In 2 hours, you'll shed a pound.

The average life span of scalp hair is about 2 to 5 years. Eyelash hairs last about 4 months only.

How come karate experts don't wreck their hands when smashing concrete slabs?

The answer is that human bones move under impact and pass part of the stress to neighboring muscles and other tissues. So the force needed to break a bone is almost 40 times greater than required to break concrete.

The skin, which is about 1/20 of an inch thick and weighs about 6 pounds, is the largest organ of the body. An average-size adult has about 18 square feet of it.

If you haven't noticed any differences lately between men and women, these findings by 2 Stanford University scientists may be of aid.

Women have keener hearing (though they are less able to tolerate loud noises), see better at night, and are more sensitive to taste and touch.

Men have faster reaction times, see better in the daytime, and are less sensitive to extreme heat, but more sensitive to extreme cold.

Doctors at Children's Hospital in Sheffield, England, pioneered a treatment for children who've lost a fingertip. In several cases, a new tip has grown back complete with sensation, nail, and even fingerprint.

The tiniest terrorist of them all—afflicting humans with misery, death, and the common cold—is the virus. Yet 3 thousand million billion of them would scarcely weigh an ounce.

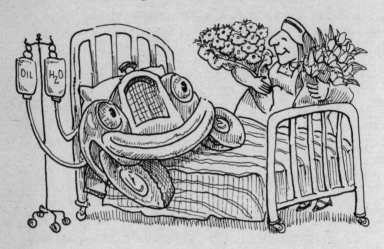

Americans spend more money caring for their cars and trucks than for their health.

The figures in 1977, according to the Hertz Corporation, were: car and truck repairs, $376 billion; medical bills for men, women, and children, $160 billion.

Rent a healthy car.

Shall we tense? . . .

In response to stress, the heart and lungs pump about 10 times the amount of blood and air we need when we are relaxed.

I WOULD JOG, BUT I DON'T KNOW HOW TO.

Boy, oh, boy: Male infants during the first 2 days of life are generally more active than female infants. But no one knows yet if the high activity is an advantage later.

Most of what we see of each other—hair and skin —is dead.

Norwegian women live longer than everyone else —an average of 77.8 years.

Your heart weighs less than a pound. Yet it pumps 2,000 gallons of blood a day and 55 million gallons in a lifetime.

A recent study found that teen-agers with a high rate of self-control and who abide by social conventions have the best chance of enjoying good health when they are in their 40s and 50s.

Smell is the least developed of human senses. Yet the memory of an odor lasts longer than the memory of a sight or a sound.
Of course. I remember it smell.

In New York City, people bite other people more often than rats bite people.

Don't cell it short: Although every cell in your body has its specialty, each is capable of developing into a complete person.

You've heard stories about men and women who are so frightened their hair turns white.
It happens, though probably not the way you think.
Older grown-ups have a mixture of black (or blond or red) hair and white. The black hair, being older hair, may fall out suddenly following a shock. Only the white is left.

Patients who are seriously ill never yawn. Nurses take yawning as a sign that the critical point has been passed. Ho-hum.

You blink once every 2 to 10 seconds. So you have your eyes shut about 30 minutes in every waking day.

With a single normal breath, you take in a pint of air—about 14 pints every minute.

Fat lot of good. . . .
Americans between the ages of 18 and 79 were collectively 2.3 billion pounds overweight in 1975.
The energy required to sustain all that extra fat would provide the yearly electrical needs of all the homes in Boston, Chicago, San Francisco, and Washington, D.C., according to 2 scientists at the University of Illinois.

You have more than 600 muscles, which total about 40 percent of your body weight.

PATIENCE, FRIENDS, DINNER IS DEFROSTING.

Blood donors are needed because nearly 22,000 pints of blood are used daily in the United States.

Blood can be stored 21 days only—unless it is frozen. But frozen blood must be used within 24 hours after defreezing.

It's enough to make your blood run cold.

The Chinese wore sunglasses 14 centuries ago.

Researchers in Chicago found it took an average

of 6.22 milliamperes (units) of electricity to make volunteers shout "ouch!" in the morning.

But in the afternoon, it took only 5.61 milliamperes.

Moral: See your dentist in the morning.

Look, don't touch: Although you have 5 senses, you receive 90 percent of your information through your sense of sight.

The best paid American doctors in private practice are obstetricians and gynecologists, followed by surgeons, internists, pediatricians, and general practitioners, according to a medical magazine.

Working mothers who are unhappy in sales and

clerical jobs are twice as likely to develop heart ailments as homemakers.

Every second, our senses send about 100 million different messages to our brain.

"Little girls are made of sugar and spice and everything nice " goes the old saying.

The U.S. Food and Drug Administration disagrees. There isn't any spice.

But the average, fully grown girl does have plenty of sugar—4 pounds of it. And a lot more.

Such as: 3 pounds of calcium; 24 pounds of carbon; 50 quarts of water; 85 pounds of oxygen; enough phosphorus for 20,000 match heads; enough chlorine to treat 5 swimming pools; enough iron for a large nail; enough fat for 10 bars of soap; enough sulphur to cure a dog of a bad case of fleas; and enough glycerine to make a good-size bomb.

A muscle does only one thing—contract.

In 1920 there were only 65 black women doctors in all the United States.

Housemaid's knee, a pre-World War II affliction, disappeared when the housemaid disappeared. It's now called sinner's knee.

People who live in high altitudes are exposed to about twice as much cosmic radiation as those who live near sea level.

And people who dwell in concrete block houses have 20 percent more radiation exposure than those in wood houses because concrete blocks contain radioactive isotopes.

Fried pimples: Teen-agers who work in fast-food restaurants and have constant contact with hot cooking oils and grease may develop a new form of acne. It's dubbed "McDonald's Acne."

Your fingertips have 2,000 pores per square inch.

Of the 15 leading causes of death in this country, men have a higher rate in 14 of them, and they're almost even with women on the 15th, according to Dr. Estelle Ramey of Georgetown University.

Modern blood tests can diagnose 2,000 different diseases.

Dark-eyed people react more quickly than light-eyed people.

Experts on the subject say you can't burn up more than 12 calories per kiss. At that rate you'll have to plant 250 smackers to lose 1 pound.
Stick to gardening.
Hoe . . . hoe . . . hoe!

Babies who learn to swim at a very early age develop into superior all-around individuals, according to a 10-year study by a team of West German doctors, teachers, and psychologists.

They also don't drown.

The longest operation, 47 hours, was performed on James Boydston, 24, of Des Moines, Iowa, to correct a flaw in his arteries. The operation started at 7 A.M. on June 15, 1979, and was completed at 6 A.M. on June 17.

Between 32 and 36 percent of the world's population have perfect 20–20 vision.

Men go bald more often than women because hair loss results when the body produces too much of the male sex hormone dihydrotestosterone.

A University of Michigan study reported in 1979 that lefties are heavier cigarette smokers than righties.

It all has something to do with the problems of getting along in a right-handed world.

The 206 bones of your skeleton make up 18 percent of your body weight.

A sneeze creates about 15 seconds of snorting and grimacing. During that time, a driver traveling at 55 miles per hour is partially blinded and dazed for about 403 yards, endangering himself and others.

Best ways to stifle a sneeze on the road are to press a finger against the upper lip or smack the thigh soundly, advises the American Automobile Association.

Or forget Sneezy, and let Grumpy do the driving.

The 25 joints of the hand give it 58 different movements.

More colds begin on Monday than any other day of the week.

Although the brain sends pain signals to the rest of the body, it has no pain sensors of its own and therefore is not itself sensitive to pain.

Hair today, gone tomorrow. . . .

The average man's beard contains 15,500 hairs which grow 15/1000 of an inch daily or 5½ inches a year.

During his lifetime, he will spend 3,350 hours shaving off 27½ feet of whiskers at the rate of a pound of hair every 16 years.

Why doesn't someone open a shavings bank?

Nearly half the people in the United States over the age of 3 wear eyeglasses.

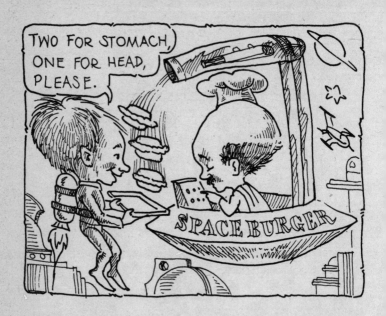

Scientists believe that 900,000 years from now the human brain will be 6.25 times its present size and use one-third of the body's energy.

Look, Ma, no drills: John Greenwood of New York City invented the dentist's drill in 1790.

Gold used in dentistry has to be soft and workable. Dentists once softened gold coins by leaving them on the railroad track till a train ran over them.

Your nose stops up when you're feeling romantic, opens when you're angry or afraid, and may be constantly stuffy when you're in low spirits.

Short men (5 feet 8 inches and under) live longer on the average than tall men (6 feet and over), according to a 1978 study reported in *Science Digest*.

Milk-crazed delinquents: A study of juvenile law-breakers discovered that hundreds of repeat offenders drank an average of twelve to fifteen 8-ounce glasses of milk a day.

Is milk bad—at least in large amounts? One theory is that the preservatives BHA and BHT affect conduct.

When gasoline soared toward $2 a gallon in 1980, everyone complained. The same year no one wrote his congressman about the cost of nasal spray. How come? The stuff cost $510 a gallon.

You wouldn't have as much fun as you think if you became invisible. You'd be blind.

The eye, being transparent, would be unable to absorb and bend light to form images.

Reading, Writing, and...Really?

A computer at the University of Akron was programmed in 1974 to refuse instructions using naughty language.

Mary Bakunin, a reading specialist in Stamford, Connecticut, can read, write, and speak backward as easily as forward.

What "the quick brown fox" is for you is "eht kciuq nworb xof" for her.

Well, that's all very easy for her to say. Tub nac ehs od gnol noisivid?

Alex Smith, 13, who won a blue ribbon at the 1979 North Carolina State Fair for his homemade muffins, had an unusual reason for taking up his hobby.

"I was having trouble in school with math," he explained. "So I started baking because it uses lots of fractions."

Some parents in Austin, Texas, coached their kids in 1979 to answer questions with, "I don't know," in order to flunk the kindergarten screening test.

Kids who failed were considered educationally handicapped and could attend class free.

A New York City psychiatrist announced in 1973 that kids who spell poorly are more likely to become criminals than kids who spell well.

Good-looking high school students receive higher grades than less attractive students, an Indiana State University study indicates.

Furthermore, girls regularly get better grades than boys of equal ability.

More than half of all United States schoolchildren have mothers who go off to jobs and aren't home after school.

A dillar, a dollar, a 2-cents scholar. . . .

A million dollars doesn't go far. If spread among the country's 43 million school kids, it would put only about 2 cents into the pocket of every pupil.

A basic skills test was given in 1977 to 465,000 Florida elementary and high school students. Third graders had the lowest failure rate. Eighth graders had the highest.

Dr. Peter Huttenlocher of the University of Chicago discovered that babies 1 and 2 years old have 50 percent more nerve connection in the cortex—the thinking area of the brain—than grown-ups.

This doesn't make them smarter than grown-ups, he says, but it might explain their better learning ability.

School vandalism is costing $600 million a year in repairs.

One out of 3 adults in the world cannot read, write, or do a simple sum in writing.

Are you reading this?

Bill Forstchen, a high school teacher in Vassalboro, Maine, decided to conduct an object lesson in American history.

In 1979 he asked his students to get signatures for a petition to repeal the "crime-coddling" first 10 Amendments to the Constitution.

More than 70 percent of the people approached signed the petitions to repeal the Bill of Rights.

Forstchen burned the petitions.

What's in your hair may have to do with how smart you are, suggests Professor Adon A. Gordus of the University of Michigan.

After studying 800 hair samples in 1973, he concluded that smart people have high amounts of zinc and copper in their locks.

The greatest single use of buses in the United States is for transporting school kids.

Yale University has a file of more than 7,000 persons who have come to its attention for falsely claiming to be alumni.

The first punctuation mark appeared in manuscripts around 364 B.C. It was a mark that separated each word from the word following.

Laugh it up. . . .

"Classes with clowns in them tend to be more productive," says Professor Sandra Damico of the University of Florida.

About three-fourths of the class clowns are a good influence. Their humor acts as a tension breaker, she claims.

Most clowns are confident and at ease in the classroom. They view themselves as leaders, but have a lower opinion than other pupils of authority figures such as teachers and administrators.

The hotbed of 1-room schoolhouses is Nebraska. At the turn of the 20th century, the United States had 200,000 1-roomers. By 1979 there were only 1,111. Nebraska boasted 431.

Richard Chamberlain, a third-grade teacher in Buffalo, New York, gives his pupils juggling breaks.

He claims juggling improves muscle control, results in good penmanship, and relieves tensions.

"You can't juggle and worry at the same time," he says.

Students academically below average are more likely to be victims of school crime.

A court ruling in 1972 upheld the right of a Sacramento (California) business college to prevent Willard Jackson from wearing his nose ornament to class.

The costliest hyphen (-) in history was the one a mathematician left out of the first Mariner-Venus space mission in 1962.

The tiny symbol represented an entire control formula. And because it wasn't there, the Atlas-Agena B rocket rolled off course shortly after take-off on July 22.

The $18,500,000 spacecraft had to be destroyed by the range safety officer.

Dash it all!

Making contact: A study of teen-agers who switched from glasses to contact lenses turned up some eye-opening facts. Sixty-six percent of the boys and girls reported better social and athletic lives. Sixty percent got higher grades.

Students from broken homes are absent twice as often as children living with natural parents. And students who ride in buses are absent less frequently than those who walk or ride in cars.

The low cost of education: Any adult can open a private school in Florida by plunking down $15 for a license.

Every month 6,000 teachers are robbed in the nation's junior and senior high schools.

People who read books participate in more leisure-time activities than do people who never read books.

Mouth-to-hand. . . .

Scientists at Swansea University in Wales found that 80 percent of the life-science students that were studied could roll their tongues into lengthwise tubes. Only 65 percent of the art students could.

Conclusion: There is a relationship between the genes that encourage people to become scientists and those that control tongue-rolling.

And now for the eyes.

Other Swansea scientists found that listeners whose eyes shift to the right when asked a question

are likely to have minds that enjoy science and mathematics.

Leftward eye-shifters are more apt to prefer the humanities.

Families around the world pay more in taxes to support the arms race than to educate their children.

Children start school knowing about 6,000 words.

To be or not TV. . . .
Many high school graduates have spent 15,000 hours watching television, but only 11,000 hours in the classroom.

Girls usually do worse than boys on true-false tests, but better on essay-type tests.

On June 25, 1678, Elna Cornaro, 32, was acclaimed master and doctor of philosophy at Padua (Italy) University. She thus became the first woman in the world to be graduated from a university.

Described as "beautiful as an angel," she wore a laurel crown on her head, a ring on her finger, and an ermine cape for the ceremony in the city's cathedral.

A Venetian noblewoman, she could speak and write in several languages and converse learnedly in philosophy, theology, mathematics, and astronomy.

One out of every eight 17-year-olds in the United States in 1977 was unable to read well enough "to perform tasks necessary to function in American society," according to the National Assessment of Educational Progress.

Ah, have a heart! Schoolteachers receive more valentines than anyone else.

Chewnior year: Students at Mt. Vernon High School in Alexandria, Virginia, lost a fight in 1979 to be allowed to chew indoors.
"Can you really imagine letting a kid chew tobacco and spit into a cup in class?" asked an astounded school administrator.

In 1928 women made up 55 percent of the elementary school principals. By 1973 they accounted for less than 20 percent. As teachers, though, women still outnumbered men by nearly 5 to 1.

Look, see the golf club: The University of Massachusetts at Amherst has a Leisure Studies department. Students are breaking down the doors to enroll in courses like "Philosophy of Leisure," "Introduction to Recreation," and "Leisure Activity Analysis."

American girls 12 to 17 years of age average 80 minutes of reading daily. Boys the same age average less than an hour.

In 1972 6 young Navajos became the first graduates of Chinle, Arizona, Rough Rock School for Medicine Men.

And you say you're the seventh son of a seventh son?

An intelligence test given to 400,000 19-year-old men in the Netherlands turned up the fact that as birth position fell, the scores on the test fell, no matter what the size of the family.

First-borns almost always did better than second-borns; second-borns did better than third-borns; third-borns did better than fourth-borns; and so on down the birth order.

The higher your education, the lower is your likelihood of being a smoker.

Susan Mills of Newberry, South Carolina, won the South Carolina United Teenager Pageant, represented her state in the national 4-H Congress, and was sent to Europe with an American leadership tour.

Moreover, as a senior at Mid-Carolina High School, she maintained top grades and planned to enter Clemson University.

But in May, 1978, she was informed that she could not graduate. In pursuing her extracurricular activities, she had missed 35 days of school.

If you miss 30 days in South Carolina, you automatically fail.

For 3 points, anyone, what's the moral?

The mother, father, and daughter of William Shakespeare, the great English poet and dramatist, could not write a word.

When Pantheon Books accepted *How the World Began* for publication in 1963, the author, Dorothy Straight, was 5 years old.

High school students buy an average of 3½ candy bars and 3 soft drinks per month from vending machines.

The shortest correspondence was between French author Victor Hugo and his publisher. Hugo wanted to know how his new novel, *Les Misérables*, was selling.

He wrote: "?"

The publisher replied: "!"

John Honey, a high school teacher in Fairfield, Connecticut, wanted to prove to his class how small were the chances of winning a state lottery. In 1978 he bought 24 tickets for the class. Twenty-three lost.

The twenty-fourth won $1,000.

First-year teachers in the Dallas school system took a test of basic skills in 1978. One out of 3 among the 535 tested did worse than the average high school junior in English and mathematics.

Flabbergasting Facts

Enough newspaper pages are printed each year to blanket the original 13 colonies.

Canadian military forces based in Trenton, Ontario, announced a moustache-growing contest in 1973. Twelve women entered.

Jeremy Jenkins, an architect in Toronto, Canada, designed an igloo made of imitation wood coated with polyurethane. In 1973 Eskimos of Hudson Bay bought one.

How long is a billionth of a second? Figure it this way: There are as many of them in a second as there are seconds in 30 years.

Hong Kong is the noisiest city in the world. What?

Lead is the most recycled raw material.

For 6 million people in the United States, English is the second language.

Without our sun, the temperature on earth would fall to minus 459 degrees Fahrenheit. All life would cease. Steel and iron would splinter and crumble at the slightest jar.

Before you rush out to buy earmuffs, cool it. The sun has another 5 billion years of life.

The tropical rain forests are being destroyed at the rate of 27 million acres a year, or 50 acres per minute.

The *Galaxy*, the largest airplane built in the 1970s, can carry 3,222,857 tortillas or 76,216 bottles of wine. If all that gives you a headache, the *Galaxy* can also carry 328,301,674 aspirin tablets.

The people of Stelle, Illinois, believe that on May 5 in the year 2000 earthquakes and volcanoes will destroy most of the earth.

They plan to float above the disaster in airships and then head to a new city in the Pacific called Philadelphia.

Floor space in the 19,201 shopping centers in the United States in 1979 could cover Manhattan Island 3½ times.

The cable address of Scotland Yard is HANDCUFFS, LONDON.

Ah, so many: Japanese publishers put out more than a billion books in 1978. That's almost 10 books for every one of Japan's 115 million citizens.

Line-gevity: A pencil will make a line 35 miles long, write more than 45,000 words, and undergo 17 sharpenings before it's worn down to 2 inches.

Half the 5 million people of Denmark share 14 family names. And 60 percent of all Danish names end in "sen."

Spare the rod. . . .

The year 1979 was the International Year of the Child, and on July 1 Sweden passed a law making it illegal for parents to strike or humiliate their children.

Spanking is now a no-no in the land of the Vikings. Papa can't cut off little Britta's TV time; Mama can't send brother Bertil to bed without supper for playing with matches.

A slip of hand or lip and it's off to family court.

THINK, NOW...
IS YOUR REQUEST
GOING TO BE
HUMILIATING?

The American Revolution cost the fledgling United States Government about $135 million. That's less than the sum budgeted for developing a fighter plane today.

A second is defined as 1/31,536,000 of the time the earth requires for a complete orbit of the sun.
And a first?

When a person becomes 80 years old, the FBI destroys his fingerprint record. As of 1979, the bureau had more than 169 million fingerprints on file.

The Department of Commerce announced that the nation's population had reached 220 million at precisely 10:45 A.M. on February 5, 1979.

The figure was an estimate, based upon a birth every 10 seconds, a death every 16 seconds, a new immigrant every 77 seconds, an emigrant departing every 15 minutes. All that equals 1 new American every 19 seconds.

The average person walks 65,000 miles in a lifetime.

Most of it to the refrigerator.

One United States family in 7 lacks a father. And on an average day, some 21,000 children are separated from their mothers because the mothers are in jail.

High tide: Trees can move water from their roots to their topmost leaves at a speed of up to an inch a second.

Senator William Proxmire of Wisconsin, a staunch foe of wasting taxpayers' money, cited as his 3 favorite examples of nonsensical federal spending: $46,000 to find out how long it takes to cook breakfast; $103,000 to study whether fish that drink tequila are more aggressive than fish that drink gin; $27,000 to determine why inmates wish to escape from jail.

The Dutch add about 12 square miles each year to their country by reclaiming the land from the sea.

Done to a turn: It takes 8,000 folds to wear out a dollar bill. European money is ready for the furnace after 2,000.

Bar none: The number of prisoners in state and federal prisons totaled 287,358 at the beginning of 1978.

Note to weight watchers: Earth's atmosphere weighs 5 quadrillion 157 trillion tons, according to the Soviet computer Minsk-22.

Mrs. Deborah Schneider of Minneapolis, Minnesota, wrote 25 words in 1958 to complete a sentence lauding the virtues of Plymouth cars.

She was awarded the contest's grand prize over a million other entrants—$500 a month for life. If she lives her expected life span, that figures to $12,000 per word.

An article on the cure of diseases in horses covered 39 pages in the first edition of the *Encyclopaedia Britannica* (1768–1771). The entry devoted to "Woman" required 4 words: "The female of man."

Ten cities across the nation can boast more telephones than people. Tops is Washington, D.C., with 150 telephones for every 100 residents.

The taxi fare from New York City to Miami, Florida, was $967.87, not including tip, in 1978. The 1,370-mile trip took 2½ days.

Pass the hot chocolate: Glaciers and ice fields cover 28,000 square miles of Alaska. That is an area about the size of South Carolina, but only 4.9 percent of the forty-ninth state.

There was enough steel in the steel corsets donated by American women during World War I to have built 2 battleships.
Of corset.

Since January 1, 1958, the United States has been kept on time by a $300,000 atomic machine that is accurate to within 1 second in 370,000 years.

The superclock is maintained by a staff of 60 in the Time and Frequency Division of the National Bureau of Standards.

It's already obsolete. Scientists at the Smithsonian Institution have built a hydrogen maser clock, which gains or loses only a single second every 50 million years.

Since you asked, yes, the earth is slowing down. In 600,000,000 B.C. a day was only 21 hours.

JUST DON'T GET AROUND AS MUCH THESE DAYS.

Mom's the word: Anna Jarvis of Philadelphia, who founded Mother's Day in the United States in 1914, never married and was not a mother. She celebrated the first Mother's Day in church.

She died in 1948, disheartened that business people were encouraging kids to believe that the only way to honor Mother was to spend money on her.

More planes are lost and never recovered over the continental United States than disappear over the Bermuda Triangle.

The motion picture *Star Wars* was the popcorn champion of all time. Theaters that usually sold 150 pounds of popcorn a week sold 1,200 pounds during the *Star Wars* showing.

"People became so nervous watching the picture that they ate like mad," said a popcorn maker.

Houston leads the nation in checks that bounce (no funds). Dallas is second, Denver is third, and San Francisco is fourth.

There are an estimated 3.2 million Smiths in the world, compared with 75 million named Chang.

In 1899 Mrs. John Howell Phillips of Chicago, Illinois, became the first woman to be issued a driver's license.

If all the paperwork spewed out by the federal government each year were dumped into Yankee Stadium, it would cover the playing field to the topmost seats 51 times.

Just be thankful you don't have a billion dollars that you *must* spend. It would take you 100 years to polish off a billion-dollar roll even if you spent $1,000 an hour, 24 hours a day, 365 days a year.

It's enough to keep a fellow awake at night.

The average American kid 2 to 5 years old watches about 20,000 television commercials a year.

Because of poor air-pollution controls, the acidity of rain is now 100 to 1,000 times normal level. A rainstorm that smacked Scotland in 1974 had as much acidity as vinegar.

The average American one-way car ride covers 10 miles for business, 12 miles for a social visit, 4 to 5 miles for a shopping trip, and 160 miles for vacation.

When Thomas Edison invented movies, he was less than enthusiastic about the building and sale of projectors. Movies, he believed, were a fad, and the novelty would soon wear off.

In a single second, light, which travels at 186,282 miles a second, can circle the earth nearly 7½ times.

A toilet seat designed to prevent people from standing upon it was patented in 1869.

Want to become a millionaire? Your best chance is in Idaho. The state has 1 millionaire in every 40 residents compared to 1 in 400 nationally.

The all-time inflation record holder is Hungary where, in 1946, 100,000,000,000,000,000,000,000 pengö bills were worth about $10.

An ounce of gold can be stretched into a wire long enough to reach halfway from Philadelphia to New York City.

113

The letters SOS don't mean "Save Our Ship." They stand for plain old *help!* The letters were chosen because they were easy to send in Morse code.

Of the 100 billion pieces of mail handled by the postal service each year, only 3.5 billion are personal letters.

Customers who bought the first Kodak camera had to mail them back to the firm in Rochester, New York, for reloading.

Most of the land—58 percent—in the United States is owned by individuals. The Federal Government owns 34 percent. States, counties, and local communities own 6 percent. American Indians own what's left, 2 percent.

American automobile makers recalled more cars than they sold in 1977. About 10.4 million passenger cars, dating back several years, were recalled; 9.3 million new cars were sold.

Newspaper tycoon William Randolph Hearst announced in his *New York Journal* that on October 17, 1896, he would run for the first time anywhere an entire comic section and, what's more, in *color*.

It would be, he proclaimed, "eight pages of polychromatic effulgence that makes the rainbow look like a lead pipe."

All portraits on United States coins face left—except Lincoln's on the penny.

Pick 'em: America's favorite flower is the rose, with the daisy second, asserts the Florists Transworld Delivery Association.

America's favorite garden flower is the zinnia, with the marigold second, asserts the National Garden Bureau.

Police say that 90 percent of all burglaries are committed by persons 13 to 21 years old.

Our known universe is becoming larger at the rate of 40 trillion cubic light-years a second.

Small kids who listen to television even when they're not watching tend to perk up when a woman's voice comes on. They pay no attention when the voice is a man's.

That, at any rate, is the finding of a research group at the University of Massachusetts. To tots, a baritone is Dullsville.

TV performers in 1980 who had to shave their heads or grow a moustache were entitled by contract to $30 in addition to their regular pay.

And extras working on TV commercials in New York had to be paid a bonus of $17.33 a day if they got wet. The sum applied to natural or artificial snow or smoke as well.

Green-yellow is the safest color for a car. It's the most highly visible color under most road conditions.

Peg o' my heart. . . .

If you sometimes feel like a square peg trying to fit into a round hole, take heart. The Government has developed a drill that makes square holes.

spirin Alley

It has become the fashion for writers to gild with importance people who are no more than good-looking or wealthy.

But what about the underdog? The innocent victim? The bonehead and the bemused? Too long have they been denied a sip of fame.

In an effort to correct such injustices, Aspirin Alley welcomes:

—Audrey Hughes, 7, of Vernal, Utah, who, missing for 2 days in the Ashley National Forest in 1979, said she saw a few of the 300 searchers pass by her. She didn't hail them because she had learned in school "not to talk to strangers."

—Sarel Goosen, 14, of Johannesburg, South Africa, who in 1979 was thrown against a fence by Jackie, a circus elephant. Regaining his senses, the boy hurried on to school and asked to be excused from taking a test, pleading a headache.

Question: How did you get the headache?

Answer: An elephant threw me against a fence as I was walking to school.

He took the test.

—The councilmen of Helsinki, Finland, who, at the urging of the city's youth committee, banned a Donald Duck comic book (*Aku Ankka*) from youth club libraries in 1978.

The young people objected to Donald's racy style of life, which included running around in a sailor suit that didn't cover his feathery bottom.

—John L. Sagers, who built a $190,000 home in a suburb of New Orleans, Louisiana. The house was 2 weeks from completion on January 14, 1977, when he discovered he had built on the wrong lot.

—Downy Ferrer of Laguna Hills, California, who bent over to kiss her turtle, a winner in a turtle race in Newport Beach in 1979. The turtle, known simply as Number 6, snapped its jaws around her upper lip and wouldn't let go.

It took 2 paramedics and a shot of Valium to unlock old Number 6. Ferrer rewarded the paramedics with her trophy and thanked them with a slight lisp.

I'LL SAY HE'S FAST! KISSING IN PUBLIC LIKE THAT!

—Georgia prison officials, who in 1978 felt that prisoners shouldn't have to look like prisoners. So they changed the uniforms to blue jeans and cotton work shirts.

Grateful visitors took to wearing matching clothes, and "too many" prisoners, mingling with friends and relatives, walked out of the gates with them.

—The New York City Fire Department, which must learn to live with tourists from Britain and some of its former colonies.

Such visitors frequently mistake a call box for a mail drop because of the red color. They insert a letter and pull the handle, just like home.

—Saudi Arabia, which in 1978 ordered 5 tons of sand from a Dutch company because its own almost limitless supply was unsuitable for the job—filtering swimming pool water.

—Kenneth Emerson of Seattle, Washington, who in 1979 abandoned his car while in pursuit of a jewelry store robbery suspect. The frightened suspect dropped $100,000 in loot. Emerson got a parking ticket.

—Pro golfer Mac McLendon, who after the first round of the 1979 Masters Tournament told his wife, Joan: "I'm playing so poorly, I just know I'm going to hit someone."

The someone was Joan, whom he hit the next morning with his tee shot on the first hole.

—Tom Clark, who was driving along U.S. 33 near Norton, West Virginia, in 1979, when he decided to conserve gas by coasting a spell. He turned off the ignition.

"The steering wheel locked," he explained from a hospital bed.

—Stephen Sharp of Cornwall, England, who by the end of 1979 had shelled out $300 to pay for his dog's munchies.

The dog, a 150-pound Great Pyrenees named Rollo, had eaten off 15 automobile mirrors, including 2 from a police car.

—James Lawrence of Omaha, Nebraska, who insisted in 1978 that he needed lots of open space to practice in.

The officer who wrote out the ticket for the $100 fine announced, gravely, that Lawrence had been warned once before about playing golf in Evergreen Cemetery.

—The 796 members of the World Stamp Collectors' Society who in 1979 went to Norwalk, Connecticut, instead of Norwalk, California, for the annual convention because of a printer's error on the invitation.

—Jack Yaun of Durand, Illinois, who, one dim and early morning in 1978, saw in the doorway of his barn the same old stray cat that had been moseying around for days.

Yaun gave it a good kick before noticing the white stripe down its back. The skunk retaliated.

"It's a hell of an experience," said Yaun. "Everybody ought to have it happen to him once."

—The 3 brick stackers at the London Brick Company in England who were suspended and fined in 1978 for coming to work 10 minutes *early*.

—Sam Gilliam, whose abstract oil painting was mistaken for a splattered dropcloth by workmen in the Richard B. Russell Federal Building in Atlanta, Georgia, in 1979.

—The woman who indignantly reported a man praying in the ladies' room at the state Capitol in Madison, Wisconsin, in 1979. Puzzled guards heard him praying in the men's room, too.

A phantom of flush?

Uh-uh. Speakers had been newly placed in the rest rooms so that representatives could keep abreast of the legislative debate when away from the chamber.

What the woman heard was the morning prayer of the Assembly.

—Hunters in New York State who in 1977 killed 83,204 deer; 1,369 wild turkeys; 551 black bears; and 7 of themselves.

—Rickey Wilson, 18, who in 1979 learned that England's get-tough policy with rowdy fans was for real. A Birmingham magistrate fined him 400 pounds —about $800—for throwing a peanut at rival supporters during a soccer game.

—Muhammad Ali, whose jaunt through the People's Republic of China in December, 1979, fell as flat as some of his opponents.

No one, apparently, had told the ex-heavyweight champion that China had outlawed boxing 20 years before as a "brutal and decadent" Western sport.

—William M. Michini, a Philadelphia fireman, who was suspended for wearing his curly blond hair too long. In 1973 he took his case to court.

"Hair," he told the judge, "does nothing more than singe."

To dramatize his point, he lighted a match and held it to his lengthy tresses, which promptly went up in smoke.

—Erwin Kreuz, a brewery worker, who in 1977 got off a plane from his native West Germany at a fuel stopover in Bangor, Maine, thinking he had arrived at his destination, San Francisco, California.

After vacationing 3 days, Kreuz, who spoke no English, stepped into a taxicab, made known his wish to be driven to downtown San Francisco, and found he could not afford the fare.

—La Verne Anne Harris, a Las Vegas grandmother, who won the world championship chili-making contest in 1978 and was awarded a trophy inscribed: "King of Chili."

—The A.A.A.A. Aaabaaabaaabee Driving School, which lost out to the A.A.A.A. Aaabaaabaaaalana Motor School in the eye-wrenching battle for top listing among driving schools in the 1979 Melbourne, Australia, telephone directory.

128

—The male choir of St. Mawgan Methodist Church in St. Mawgan, England, which didn't just stand there singing "When Stars Begin to Fall" in January, 1980. They fell themselves.

In the middle of the hymn, the rotting floorboards of the choir loft gave way, dropping the singers upon the parishioners below. No one was hurt.

—The city council of Woonsocket, Rhode Island, which in 1978 renamed the town's manholes in a frenzied drive to eliminate sexism. The new name: personholes.

—Paul Rannenberg, luncheon director of the schools in Springfield, Massachusetts, who in 1979 got a complaint signed by every second grader at Lincoln Elementary.

The kids had worked hard all week preparing to recreate the Pilgrims' Thanksgiving Day feast. Rannenberg forgot to order the turkey.

The small Pilgrims had to eat hot dogs.

—Prince Charles of England, who in 1978 was asked, "Why do you always stand with your hands behind your back?"

Replied the prince: "My father does it, too, but it's not a habit I picked up from him. The reason lies with our tailor. We both share the same one. He makes the sleeves so snug, we have a hard time keeping our hands in front."

—William Smith of Waukegan, Illinois, who never had a chance to celebrate his election as Lake County auditor in 1978. On the same day voters abolished the job.

—Katie Crowe, a tourist from Carollton, Texas, who landed a trophy-size sailfish in 1979 that "seemed kind of lifeless."

More than kind of.

A mate aboard the Miami Beach charter boat had secretly fixed a dead fish to her hook, after which Mrs. Crowe was talked into having her "catch" mounted. Normal kickback on a mounting fee—30 percent to the crew.

—Andrew Bavas, who in 1978 declared, "I guess I've got no future as a Government bureaucrat." He came under so much flak for refusing a pay increase from the Department of Health, Education, and Welfare that he decided to resign.

—Ralph Wagner of Miami, Florida, who in 1979 injured his leg kicking a vending machine. He sued the manufacturer for $200,000 for failing to make machines safe for people to kick.

—And Carl C. Lane of Cusseta, Georgia, who was too enraged to kick a vending box that swallowed his 50 cents but didn't give him a Sunday newspaper in 1980.

Instead, he held the $190 box hostage in his home for 3 days.

—The firefighters at the Stratford, Connecticut, headquarters, who had their ups and downs getting out of the firehouse in 1979. When they leaped aboard their engine, the overhead door closed.

The company that installed the door found the trouble. The frequency of the automatic opening device was the same as the one on the fire truck radio. On went the radio, down came the door.

—Shannon Brixey, 6, of Tulsa, Oklahoma, who in 1979 had a tooth fall out at school. Since she had no pocket to keep it in for the Tooth Fairy that night, she stuck it in her ear.

A team of doctors and nurses had to use a general anesthetic before they could rescue it for the Tooth Fairy.

—Rita Baker, who was lecturing in 1979 in Osceola, Arkansas, on what to do in a blackout—when the lights went off.

—The Allied Roofing and Siding Company of Grand Rapids, Michigan, which in 1979 was so busy removing snow from other people's roofs that it neglected its own. Yep, the roof collapsed.

—Arthur J. Kraus of Long Island, New York, who eats a clove of garlic every day for his health. In 1980 he complained that bus drivers refused to stop for him because of his bad breath.

—The Englishman who had Andy Smulion, 20, of London, for a bill collector.

On the job Andy wore a 22-year-old raincoat that had never known the cleaners. To sustain its powers of persuasion, he regularly mixed "the most repulsive stuff together" and dropped the raincoat into it.

The stench drove people wild, but Andy, with permanently blocked sinuses, didn't smell a thing.

His technique was to plop himself in reception

rooms and offices and refuse to budge till payment was made.

In 1979, before being arrested for "insulting behavior," the human stink bomb failed to collect 3 accounts only.

—Charles Allcorn, who in 1979 was fired from his job as a waiter at Wheeler's, a seaside restaurant in Brighton, England.

Among the complaints lodged against him was his inclination to spray furniture polish over cheese appetizers.

—Danielle Searcy, 2, who bounced off her bed and shot through the window of her grandparents' apartment in Southfield, Michigan, in 1978. She fell 9 stories and landed in some shrubbery, unhurt.

—Russian teen-agers, who must not only toe the party line, but wear it. In 1979 the Kremlin okayed only 2 slogans for T-shirts:"The Communist Party and the People Are One" and "Glory to Labor."

—Jonathan Sirkin, 7, of Newark, New York, who in 1979 brought his dad's handcuffs to school for show-and-tell. He forgot to bring along the key and had to be freed by police officers.

—Bill Moore of Phoenix, Arizona, who returned from a stay in the hospital in 1979 to find his house stripped bare.

County officials had misunderstood a court order to "clean up" Moore's house while he was away. They thought the order said "clean out" and hired a liquidator to auction off all Moore's possessions.

—Gerald Overstreet of Del Rio, Texas, who in 1979 reached for a jelly jar in Gibson's Discount Store and was bitten by a rattlesnake.

He sued but lost. An appeals court ruled that a store's duty to protect its customers from wild animals does not begin until the animal is known to be around.

—Barney T. Arthur, Jr., who in December, 1979, was awarded the Lynchburg (Virginia) Police Department's medal of honor. A month later he was fired for being 4 pounds overweight.

—The Citizens Committee for the Right to Keep and Bear Arms, which in 1979 sent Christmas cards to members of Congress. The card showed Santa Claus in front of a fireplace, smiling and holding a pistol.

—Alice E. Blattler, who was told she couldn't vote in the 1979 elections because town records listed her dead. She protested in vain.

Then, since dead people don't pay taxes, she didn't either. Officials quickly admitted their mistake.

But life wasn't the same. "I still meet people who want to know if I'm alive or dead," she said.

—George Dillard of Riverhead, New York, who in 1980 couldn't sleep. Hard rock music pounded through his skull at all hours of the night.

A little dental detective work found the cause: his new set of false teeth.

The metal in the bridge was picking up station

WKCI-FM in Hamden, Connecticut, 30 miles away. His jawbone was serving as an amplifier.

The false teeth went into a glass at night.

—Ivan Bright and his son Lloyd, of Hope, Arkansas, who in 1979 narrowly missed the $10,000 prize offered by the city's Tourist Commission to anyone who could grow a 200-pound watermelon.

The Brights' watermelon didn't reach 200 pounds until 3 days after the deadline.

—George Mellendorf, who, while a soldier in Vietnam, complained in a letter to President Richard Nixon:

"Dear President Nixon: It seems nobody cares if we get our mail. We are lucky to get it twice a week. Sir, someone is not doing their job."

Mellendorf penned the letter on January 4, 1971. It was delivered to Mr. Nixon in February 1978— 7 years later.

—Emperor Menlik II of Ethiopia, who ordered one of those newfangled electric chairs from America shortly before the start of the 20th century, when Ethiopia had no electricity.

So it shouldn't be a total loss, he converted the chair into a throne.

—Leonard and Edith Pearman of Hatfield, England, who complained that the back door to their Government-subsidized house leaked.

After 2 years, the Government sent workmen to paint it. The paint did not stop the leaking. So a new door was put in—backward. Moreover, it was too small.

In 1979, after workmen had made 26 visits, the Pearmans finally got the door fixed.

—Oscar Flores, governor of the Mexican state of Coahuila, who was invited to be the guest of honor at a celebration in Laredo, Texas, in 1980.

Customs officials at the border wouldn't let him into the United States because he lacked proper identification.

—Dick Winslow, who in 1979 walked into the Good Samaritan Hospital in Los Angeles, California, ticked off about a pain in his throat. Doctors

found a Mickey Mouse watch stuck in his esoph-
agus.

Winslow reckoned the watch was in a glass of
vitamin pills he had swallowed several days earlier.

—T. H. Shevlin of Minneapolis, Minnesota, who
in 1902 received the first ticket for speeding. He was
motoring along at better than 10 miles an hour.

—Grace Hemmendinger, a 6-foot-1-inch, 275-
pound professional female wrestler, who barn-
stormed across the United States from 1875 to 1878
and then joined a Wild West show as a "strongman."

The masquerade was dictated by good business
practice. Her employer didn't think the public would
take to a woman with stronger muscles than most
men's.

—The people of Montreal, Canada, who "do not
have the same discipline and sense of responsibility
that can be found in other Canadian provinces or in
different U.S. states."

So ruled city officials in turning down the appli-
cation for right turns on red lights in 1979.

—King Henry VI of England, who in 1439 sought to curb the spread of disease by banning kissing.

MS READ-a-thon— a simple way to start youngsters reading

Boys and girls between 6 and 14 can join the MS READ-a-thon and help find a cure for Multiple Sclerosis by reading books. And they get two rewards — the enjoyment of reading, and the great feeling that comes from helping others.

Parents and educators: For complete information call your local MS chapter. Or mail the coupon below.

Kids can help, too!